THE AMAZING ADVENTURES OF

CHESTER THE WIENER DOG

Chester Gets a *Furever* Family

Dr. James Kirby Easterling

innovativeink
PUBLISHING

Cover image © Shutterstock.com

www.innovativeinkpublishing.com
Send all inquiries to:
4050 Westmark Drive
Dubuque, IA 52004-1840

Published in the United States of America

Dedication

This book is about families who open their hearts &
homes to those in need for a lifetime of happiness
through the miracle of adoption.

About the Author

Dr. James Kirby Easterling—a proud Appalachian whose family has been in Kentucky for eight generations—donates his time and resources to a multitude of child advocacy agencies and animal rescue organizations. Dr. Easterling and his wife, Teresa, have three beautiful daughters and three amazing granddaughters… and seven pups of every age, shape, size, and color!

I truly hope your family enjoys the positive and encouraging message of my special little book and would be honored if you would recommend it to friends, family members, and colleagues. Be looking for more "Chester" books soon! I would love to hear from you and am available for speaking engagements and other signature events.

Contact Information:
Dr. James Kirby Easterling
KirbyEasterling@gmail.com
Call/text: 859-779-5858

Chester's Autograph

Chester

This is a story about a little dog named Chester
Who always wanted a warm little sweater!

A pup who lived in the woods all alone
Now lives in a castle home

He once was cold and had no covers
But now he's loved by 3 sisters & 3 brothers

At night he laughs
While he takes warm baths

He loves to sleep in a warm soft bed
With his loving Mother gently rubbing his head

He's black & white with a long slender body
When he wakes up early, he seems kinda groggy

His belly was once empty
But now he has plenty

His family he loves
And gives thanks to above

This is a story about a special little black & white wiener dog puppy named Chester, who has a long slender body, short legs, and floppy ears. Chester lived in a spooky wooded area bordering a country road. Chester was scared, hungry and alone. Chester really wanted a loving Mom and Dad.

A kind lady named Mrs. Howard was walking alongside the country road and found Chester and took him inside her house for a few days. The lady had lots of cats, which Chester naturally loved to chase. Mrs. Howard wanted to help Chester find a *furever* home with a loving family where he would be happier.

Chester went with Mrs. Howard to visit several families over the next few weeks, but Chester just didn't fit in. Chester was sad thinking no one wanted him. Chester wanted the perfect family to give all his slobbery wet kisses and cuddles and to be loved in return.

After taking Chester to visit multiple homes, Mrs. Howard thought of a
special family that lived in a magnificent castle that already had lots of dogs.
Chester had never seen a castle before and was so excited. The Mom and
Dad already had six dogs of every age, shape, size, and color…but they had
just enough love for one more puppy. Chester came for a visit and brought
all his clothes & toys in a suitcase and was adopted by the family.

Chester now has brothers and sisters to play with each day. The oldest dog is Tink—a small brown & white chiweenie with a loud yapping bark—and she watches Chester very closely so that he doesn't get into too much trouble with jumping on the furniture and taking the other dogs' toys. Tink was adopted as well, so she wants to make Chester feel welcome as sometimes it takes adopted puppies a few days to learn all the family rules and expectations.

Chester's brothers are Trooper, Roscoe, and Boomer. And besides Tink, his other sisters are Chee and Maggie. Chester is so excited and wants to play with the other dogs all the time. Some of the other dogs are much older, so they just rest and watch little Chester play. Sometimes Chester grabs the other dogs' toys, but sharing toys is a kind thing to do, and Chester always brings them back. All the older dogs love little Chester and are thankful that he's part of their family now.

Chester loves to play with Trooper, who is roughly the same color, but is much bigger! Trooper is Chester's big brother, and every evening the Dad throws the squeaky ball for Chester and Trooper to chase until they're tired and need a snack.

Chester loves eating breakfast with his family each morning before everyone goes to school and work. Chester's favorite breakfast meal is pancakes & maple syrup! The Mom always says *"Chester, don't eat too many pancakes or you'll get a tummy ache!"*

Chester loves looking out the window and watching for packages to be delivered. Sometimes the delivery person gives Chester a snack for being such a good puppy. Chester always pokes his long cold wet nose in each package hoping for a new squeaky ball—his favorite toy of all!

Chester and Boomer don't like to go outside when it's raining, so they have raincoats. If Chester gets wet, he simply "wiggles & jiggles" until he's dry again. Sometimes he even jumps up on the bed, and his Mom kindly says *"Chester, get off the bed and dry those cold wet feet!"*

Chester loves to rest near his Dad every evening and take a nap. Chester feels safe and loved when he's with his Dad. After a short rest, Chester is ready to chase the squeaky ball again.

Chester's new family has a huge yard with lots of trees. Chester loves to run and play outside and poke his long cold wet nose in lots of places. Chester loves to chase squirrels most of all, though he never catches any. After playing for a while with Trooper, Chester loves to lay in the grass and take warm naps!

Chester loves to take a bath each night and play with his yellow rubber ducky named Quack. Sometimes Chester accidently splashes water in the floor, and his Mom says *"Chester, it's time to get out of the bathtub and get ready for bed. We have to get up early tomorrow morning for school and work!"*

Chester loves to play with the neighborhood kids too at a nearby community park. Chester always wants to include everyone so that no one feels alone. When the kids stop playing to have a snack, Chester shares their snacks too. Chester always wants to share other's snacks!

At night Chester wears pajamas and a sleeping cap to bed to stay extra warm. Chester and his Dad have matching dinosaur pajamas. The Dad likes to relax by reading books about puppies, and Chester likes to relax and think all about people! It's good to know more about others.

Mrs. Howard periodically stops by and checks on Chester to make sure he is happy and continuing to grow bigger and stronger. Chester always remembers Mrs. Howard being kind and helping him find his furever family. Mrs. Howard always tells Chester to *"be a good puppy and listen to your new Mom and Dad and I'll be back to check on you again soon!"*

In the winter Chester loves to play outside in the snow. Chester likes to chase snowballs thrown by his Dad. Chester can run super-fast even while wearing his favorite sweater! After being outside in the cold for a while, Chester loves a big bowl of hot chocolate while resting by the castle's warm fireplace!

Chester loves his soft warm bed. Sometimes Chester's brothers and sisters sleep with him. Everyone feels safe and loved because of others sleeping nearby. Chester always sleeps with his squeaky ball.

Chester loves celebrating holidays with his family, and Christmas is his favorite time of the year. Chester likes to lay by the warm fireplace with his brothers and sisters marveling at the beautiful Christmas tree and all the shiny presents. Chester wonders if his parents have bought him a new squeaky ball! But most of all Chester wants all the other dogs to get a new toy for Christmas. Chester always thinks of others.

Chester is so thankful for his furever family. Chester says a prayer each
night before going to sleep. Chester has a warm bed, lots of food to eat,
other dogs to play with, and a loving Mom and Dad. Chester wouldn't
trade his special family for any other family in the whole world!
Every life is truly special.

Questions for Reading Comprehension

1. How would you describe Chester's ears, legs, and body?

2. What is the lady's name who found Chester?

3. What are the names of Chester's brothers and sisters?

4. What does Chester like to wear to stay warm?

5. What does Chester like to share of others?

6. What small animal does Chester like to chase around the yard?

7. What is Chester's favorite breakfast meal?

8. What's is Chester's rubber ducky's name?

9. What is Chester's favorite toy?

10. What does Chester do each night before going to sleep?

This book is in honor of my great friend—retired U.S. Navy Commander Mark E. Farris—who has transported more abandoned and neglected puppies into furever homes than anyone I've ever known.